Alien(s)

by
Yael Valencia Aldana

Sweetie Press

Hollywood,
Florida

Sweetie Press
5924 Sheridan Street, No. 2128
Hollywood, Florida, 33021
sweetiepress.com

Alien(s)/ Yael Valencia Aldana. -- 1st ed.
ISBN 979-8-9892793-0-2

To all of us Aliens in love's mire.

Table of Contents

For You
for Ricardo and Jennita

There was a time
in the pantheon
the time before quasars
the time before penumbras
were invented.
the time before souls
when we were twins clung
together—
brothers? sisters?
who knows, but one skin
one gossamer bubble
of thread, dark eye to dark eye.
the residue adheres
sticky filaments on the wing.
 it arrows, it winnows, stretches
thin as mylar.
it is the most tapered
kind of affection.

Alien Poem #10

I didn't know my mother hated
you not because your nickname
was Alien
not because you looked like Jesus
not because of your guitar picked fingers.
When I said we were getting divorced
She said,
good he's an idiot
I have never known her to hold
her tongue, not once
didn't know she could.
he's shy, I'd say.
not an idiot, I'd say
I defend you because
that's what I do
 we didn't make it
but that doesn't mean
you aren't the best person
I've met
doesn't mean
I still don't love you
doesn't mean
I won't defend you
 she said.
what could I say, you were marrying the fool?
he was sweet, I said.
he was from Vermont, I said.
he loved me how
I couldn't love him back.
my love turned brotherly
and bitter.

Single Strand

The pull of a smooth
single strand of hair
beneath my watch strap
reminds me of your coils
I find cooly tangled
in my fingers
well after you
are gone.

Alien poem #12

You are the best person I have met/not the strongest but the best/The worst thing you ever did I made you do/Drunk off our asses atop a ten story apartment roof in Brooklyn/ I command you to climb down the fire escape/ steal a tiny barbecue grill/ I see below/Game/ you climb down/you call up/ *I can't make it up with the grill/ Do it*, I slur/*Don't come up here without that fucking grill*/ I, confident in your athleticism/ You return with the grill/ Our triumph, our token, our coup.

You could have died ten stories up/ Jumping between fire escape and the roof ladder/you survived my drunken bulling/ Maybe I'm the worst person I ever met.

We take the tiny grill home/ Is it really ours?/ We never use it/ We giggle over it/ Our triumph, our token, our coup.

You are the best person I ever met/ Not the strongest but the best/ I might be the worst person you have met/ Am I your most dangerous Ex?/ Would you be in danger if I reappeared?

If I thought we could make it/ I would take you back. /Would you let me?/ I would storm into your new relationship/ leave your girlfriend in shambles/ Fuck the feminist sisterhood./ I would sent her back to her mother crying/ Back to her best friend crying. /Feminism means you need to be strong,/ So take it and I'll take him.

I have been that bitch and I would have been that bitch again/ I would have taken the karma and I would have taken you/ But we wouldn't have made it./ So I let you alone.

To Watch Her Face Fall

I

I am wounded
my washi thin skin darkens with blood
frayed open flesh ragged
at the edges. I don't want
to tell her, to show her—
but she will ask.

I can bear it alone, the weight of this upset,
knit the lesion back before I see her,
continue the interlacing of fascia after
I see her, conceal the bruise
the sliced skin—
but she will ask.

I harrow then sear watching her face
crest and fall, watching
her shining shadow.
If only for a few minutes
till her face brightens,
till her mouth dances
to distract from my harm.
Our love is this silent chafing.

II

Bodily harm becomes invisible shadowing
barely darkened imperfections, a closing
over that will smooth—
return to unblemished perfection

to all eyes but ours, only us aware
of the slight scar lightly covered in hair.
Smoothing over her face that fell.
She cannot forgive because it was me
I cannot forgive because it was her—
her face that fell.

She wants to go back. Soothe
with words as slim as apple chips.
Soothe with her rhythmic voice
that rises and falls in waves.

Our faces slick over, leaving only slight
sharpening in the corners of the shields
in our eyes squinting, glinting
black metal.

She will say it's alright and not mean
it I will agree and not mean it.
We will put our glossy heads together,
 draft new plans for unnamed streets.

She will hold my hand tighter
which is the only good bit. Until I am ready
to leave the hearth of her protection
sheathed in armor we will temper
anew.

The Most Dangerous Ex

They look like brothers
Alan whose nickname is Alien
and Erik whose nickname is E.
Erik sent me a picture of himself
that looks nothing like him. I meet
him sitting in a downtown Fort
Lauderdale bar, looking at me with
Alien's face through E's brown eyes instead
of Alan's blue.

There are differences
E is taller.
Alien has perfect teeth
E is 14 years younger,
but 90 percent they are the same,
twins,
same body,
same hair,
almost the same face—
 It's frightening.

E, the dangerous one.
We, together mere months.
Alan and I together for seven years.
I drive away from E's, rubber spewing g
ravel, to counterman his drinking
his cocaine dipshits all over the house.

But when E calls me two years hence,
then 5 years hence, my heart
 swivels I strain to resist him. Why?
He is terrible.
It's not because he reminds me
of Alien. Maybe Alien reminds me
of him. It's not because he's an ass.
My phone is full of asshole exes
I don't bother to text back.
There's sticky stardust between
us, stretching like albumen binding
us in a galaxy
we have forgotten.

The adult in me resists him
admirably. While the brat in me wants only to lick
him like a lollipop. You wouldn't know how hard
her adult heart beats, how her skin prickles
when he puts his hand on her lower back when-
she-has lunch-with-E-without-telling-her-then-
current-now-recently-ex boyfriend.

E is the hook, and I am the latch.
This is the crux
Do you know what will happen?
Have you ever fallen
on sea-slicked rocks—let the ocean take
you? Watch the safety of shore slide away?
Maybe that's why he keeps coming back
like a turtle that returns to the beach where
she was born.

Miami Map

I know what is going on: he sends me a picture
shirtless lying on his bed, I see his farmer's tan.

Haven't seen him in four years. My most dangerous ex. His
eyes are bottom of the river brown reflecting, almost no light.

Eyebrows thick sabled slashes towards those eyes—
here is where you die on his altar.

I meet him at the taco place on 25th street and 2nd Ave.

I know what's going on, he leans against me looking up
at the menu deciding what to order.

Burrito de pollo? Taco de camarones?

His hand is already between my shoulders.
I read him a poem I have written.

When I say
how her skin prickles when he puts his hand on her lower back,
he moves his hand to my lower back,

meta on meta.

I know what is going on, when he easily threads his dry smooth
fingers between mine in Margaret Peace park.

We kiss on the corner at North East 17th Street and North
Miami Ave waiting for the light to change.

His tongue feels like velvet and tastes like cigarettes, a flavor
I like from my Brooklyn youth.

His purple Kangol hat falls down his back
into my hand.
He says my mouth tastes like Cocoa Macha ice cream.

The light from the street lamp plays in his eyes. They
are a clear sparrow brown.

Mud and River

When we find space we will merge together like/mud and water/River and sea.

We have started already sliding against each other like minnows/Scales rubbing/ There is a catch, a hitch, a pause/ We have nowhere to go.

He is evicting a roommate stubbornly squatting/ My living room is my bedroom. My roomate wandering through to see what I am doing.

We are furtive, grasping at mouths like gold fish for air/ His hands find my skin through the cracks of my clothes.

He is a good croucher. /He his 8 inches taller than me/ But he bends, scooches, and adjusts. I can feel the growing mound of his desire against my pubis.

I am a cleft, a maw, an inverted tube of muscle and gristle/ that wraps around his skin like the asp I am to his viper.

We always did this part well, the slipping and sliding of bodies.

Once we slept on a single mattress, the undulating sinew two adult bodies wound around each other. /don't know how we managed it.

ALIEN(S)

Hopefully he won't turn into that asshole./ Hopefully I won't turn into that needy bitch.

We are that irritating couple on the street swapping spit/ My mom used to yell get a room./ We have no room to go to.

We will wait, rimming the periphery./We can wait./ We can wait./ We can wait./ Waited five years to get this shit right.

Dick Ghazal

Would I like to come down for some tea and a side of dick?
You don't say *and a side of dick.*

But I know you mean tea
with a side of dick

This is why you ask me to your house:
for adventures with that dick.

I should say no.
Thursday would be better for a bit of dick.

But I won't. I never say no to you—
especially with a side of dick.

I'll drive over to drink the tea you make for me:
Ayurvedic loose-leaf and roasted green tea with that side of dick.

It's not really a side of dick. I also call it fucking
to act like I don't care about you, the sex and your dick.

But I do care.
It's not a fuck with a side of dick.

Its synergy manifested as a synchronic singularity—
with a side of dick.

Turgid Maw

Curved
maw, cleft,
liquid moist opening,
moisture soft now hard
turgid now pressing pushing into
petal softened tacky like taffy yielding inverted
snake muscle pulsing gripping clenching
unclenched skin sheen slick sweat hair some short
some long browner bits lighter bits parted
moisten meeting tasting touching probing
proboscis
blushed and bumpy a flushed red
velvet cake inside after the
chest rises slowly falls
slower the mystery
of morning
awaits.

I Am the Ex

I am no longer the ex.
What would she call me?
The man?
Her man?
Erik Bipolar 1.

Suppose we are not bound together like chain?
Supposed we are the chain?
This why I forgave her for slapping the glasses off my face
breaking them.

> That's why she forgave me for moving
> another woman into the house
> in front of her face.

It's the bipolar babe.

Did she forgive me?
> Is that forgivable?
> I grazed on beer all day like Cheetos

It's the bipolar babe.

> I am the asshole.
> I was the asshole.
> I was off my face.
> I loved the beers and Cheetos.

I was the bipolar babe.

She wanted things from me I couldn't give—
    didn't want to give.

I wanted to break her for pushing me,
and
I did.
        It was the bipolar babe.

        I knew she would stand there
        and take it, and she did
        until she didn't.

But I want her, wanted her,
        even when I couldn't stand her.
        My finger whorls crave her skin.

        I came back.
        It's OK, she was with some guy.

I was still off my ass—
        I would have fucked it up
        with the beer and the Cheetos,
        and the bipolar.

        I came back-I come back-I came back again.
        Doesn't that mean that I can love her?
        I will not fuck it up.
        No more beers and Cheetos
        on my meds four years straight.

We are the chain,
third time together.
                I fucked it up.

The Necromancer Returns in Distress

I have never made love
for comfort before.
my clothes come off like
wet tissue in your hands.
the soulmate fire gone,
slim hips to slim hips—
                    it is love still.
your voice vibrates
hummingbirds in my ear—
I laugh.
we look like we are in love.
we are not,
            but we love still.

I don't want to go to the late
nite BBQ place.
I go
your hand warm,
low on my back.
we have never been so easy
our knives sheathed.

dawn's tangerine clouds
brings a new month.
I watch you drive away
in your blood orange SUV—
            free.
I walk under the pink
plumeria tree to my yellow door— free
                love still.

ALIEN(S)

Yael Valencia Aldana is an award-winning poet and writer. She is the author of the poetry collection *Black Mestiza*. She is a Pushcart Prize winner, and her work has appeared in *Torch Literary Arts*, *Literary Mama*, and *Slag Glass City*, among others. She teaches creative writing in South Florida and is the managing editor of Purple Ink Press. She lives near the ocean with her son and too many pets. You can find her online at YaelAldana.com.

Acknowledgments

"Turgid Maw" was published in *Womanly Magazine*.
"To Watch Her Face Fall" was published in *Superstition Review*.
"Alien Poem #12" appeared in *Stonecoast Review*.

www.ingramcontent.com/pod-product-compliance
Lightning Source LLC
Chambersburg PA
CBHW051651120626
46551CB00015B/2320